Grow The F*ck Up

By: John Kyle

Available for sale and distribution through Ingram or buy direct through Unrefinedpublishing.com

ISBN-13: 978-1511720243

DEDICATION

I dedicate this book to my mother and father. I could not have asked for a more supportive and loving set of parents. To friends, family, and strangers that have supported my work, you are awesome. I hope you enjoy this book as much as I have loved working on it.

TABLE OF CONTENTS

ACKNOWLEDGMENTS

I do not wish to write some acknowledgement that you're sure to skim through. Instead, I would like to use this section for something more. While writing this novel, discrimination, uncanny sensitivity, and environmental dilapidation were plaguing the earth. Because some people are dicks, these issues as well as others are still occurring. Simply put, it's never too late to change the world. Start treating one another like equal human beings. Whether you're gay, straight, black, brown, Christian, or other, we are all the same on the inside. Once we learn to accept each other, we can help fix the problems that plague our planet. Let's be a better world. Together.

1

AUTOMOTIVE ADVICE

I. How to Change a Tire

Many people run into this problem at some point or another. One moment they are driving along and then their tire decides to up and take a shit on them. Be one of those people that can effectively change a tire without the help of an automotive service by using the steps outlined below.

Step 1: Get the hell off the road. It is imperative that once a tire is blown, you slowly pull off the road as far to the right as possible. Put your car into park, apply the parking brake, and turn on your hazards to alert the world that you're about to have a shitty day.

Step 2: Get out the necessary tools for the job. This includes a jack, tire iron, and spare tire. Don't fret, all of these items should have come with the vehicle. For all of you men and women that do not wish to dirty your designer clothing, you had better have a tarp and some gloves packed away in your vehicle.

Step 3: Position the jack. Place the jack under the vehicle near the tire that needs to be changed. Be sure to align the jack with the metal frame of your vehicle or else you'll end up cracking that sweet body kit of yours. On the metal frame, you should see a groove or marking that indicates where exactly to place the jack itself. If you still have no clue where to place it on your specific model of car, remove your testicles and either call a real man or proceed to explore your owner's manual for more detailed instructions.

Step 4: Get some support and loosen your nuts. Crank the jack to the point where your car is supported but not lifted off the ground. Once that is complete, you can remove the hub cap and loosen the lug nuts by using the tire iron. It is important to remember that the nuts need to be turned counterclockwise in order to be removed. If you don't know which direction counterclockwise is, stick your finger out in front of you. Starting from the top, rotate your finger to the left in a circular fashion. When you've finished, kick yourself in the head.

Step 5: Jack it up, not off. Remove the hub cap and crank the jack up in order to lift the vehicle high enough to remove the tire

and replace it with the spare. You'll be completely removing the lug nuts from the flat tire, swapping out the flat for the spare, and then reapplying the lug nuts to the spare tire once it is firmly in place. When applying the lug nuts to attach the spare tire, remember to turn them clockwise and ensure that they are on tight.

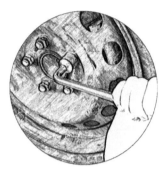

Step 6: Lower the jack and tighten your nuts. Slowly lower the jack until your new tire begins to touch the ground. Take this moment to tighten the lug nuts once more using the tire iron.

Step 7: Remove the jack. Gently lower your car until you can safely remove the jack. Again, I would advise triple checking your lug nuts, although that may be because I have a slight case of OCD. The last thing you want is to be driving and have your tire pop off, causing you to swerve into a gas tanker that ignites and slowly cooks you and your loved ones to death. But that's just my opinion.

Step 8: Stow your tools. Place the flat tire, tire iron, and jack back in the vehicle and you're good to go! Happy driving.

II. How to Change a Car Battery

Thanks to modern technology, we have car batteries that will crap out on us when we need them to function most. Need not worry, the steps outlined below will help you to change your battery while hopefully avoiding acidic burns and all that other fun, battery-related stuff.

Step 1: Gather the essentials. Ensure that you have the proper attire for dealing with corrosive materials - gloves, eye protection, and clothing that you couldn't care less about will probably be your best bet. The reason for this being that if any acid happens to get on you or your clothing, you're going to need a new wardrobe and, potentially, medical attention.

Step 2: Identify the correct replacement battery. Vehicles have different battery sizes, so either look in your owner's manual or give your car's specifications to a local auto parts store to see which battery is needed. In some cases, you can get credit for recycling an old battery when purchasing a new one (this is outlined in step 6).

Step 3: Shut off your car stereo and get to work. The battery should be located either under the hood, in the trunk, or even potentially under a seat depending on the make and model of your vehicle. Once found, locate the negative and positive terminals of the battery. The positive terminal will have a (+) symbol while the negative terminal will have a (-) symbol. If you're still having issues, find a child that just took basic math and they can help you determine which is which. Just don't approach them with a pedo mustache or you may end up becoming someone's prison bitch.

Step 4: Disconnect the negative terminal. Simply disconnect the negative terminal by loosening the attached clamp. To do so, you will need to utilize an appropriately sized wrench (generally 8mm or 10mm). You will want to completely disconnect the negative terminal first to avoid short circuiting the positive terminal.

Step 5: Disconnect the positive terminal. Disconnect the positive terminal using the same tool as outlined in step 4.

Step 6: Remove and recycle your old battery. Remove the old battery after detaching any clamps or nuts that may have been holding it in place. The battery itself may have a carry handle to make for easy removal. After removing the old battery, be sure not to lay it on its side or upside down as this could cause it to leak and corrode items in its vicinity. Better yet, throw it in a cardboard box and bring it to an auto parts store. In return for recycling your old battery, the clerk should give you a credit that is good towards a new battery. This is known as a core charge.

Step 7: Install the new battery. Place the battery in its proper location with the positive and negative terminals on the correct sides. Be sure to apply any clamps or nuts that are used to hold the battery in place. If you're not sure which way to install the battery, they typically come with an indicator stating which way it faces. The arrow should be pointing toward the front of the vehicle.

Step 8: Connect the positive terminal. Reconnect the positive terminal and tighten the clamps.

Step 9: Connect the negative terminal. Reconnect the negative terminal and tighten the clamps. When the negative terminal makes contact, it may set off your car alarm causing you to shart without warning, so just keep that in mind. If you'd need to visualize the concept, I have provided an image at the top of the next page.

Step 10: Start your engine. Close the hood, turn on your car, and ensure that all of your electronics are in working condition. Your clock and radio may have reset after the change, so just adjust them as needed.

If you failed to trade it in as outlined in step 6, be sure to recycle your old battery. The corrosive materials contained within are terrible for the environment. I don't need some unknown radioactive material leaking into a lake that I frequent causing me to grow a second dick. In other words, don't be a jackass. Grow the fuck up and take it to an auto repair shop or recycling center that will properly dispose of the battery.

III. How to Gather Information in Case of an Accident

With assholes all over the road texting and driving, it is important to know how to handle the exchange of information when a vehicular accident occurs. The five categories of information that should be gathered in the case of an accident include personal, automobile, insurance, scene, and photographic information. The details below should help you obtain most, if not all, of the necessary information.

Personal information: This includes names, home addresses, e-mail addresses, and phone numbers of everyone involved in the accident. Be sure to obtain the same information from any potential witnesses as well.

Automobile information: Write down the make, model and license plate information of all of the cars involved. You will also want to record the VIN, otherwise known as the vehicle identification number, of each vehicle. This can generally be located on the owner's vehicle registration, inside the driver's side door, or on a metal plate near the lower right side of the dashboard.

Insurance information: This includes the information regarding all other insurance companies involved. Company names, phone numbers, and policy numbers should all be recorded.

Scene information: It is important to document where and when the accident occurred. Be sure to record the location whether it is an intersection, freeway exit, or the front of an establishment, as well as the exact time that the accident occurred. If first responders arrive, obtain their information as well. This includes badge numbers, department numbers, names of with whom you speak, and vehicle numbers.

Photographic information: Thanks to advances in technology, that cell phone in your pocket that's also equipped with a camera and multiple vibration settings to tickle your asshole will be extremely useful in the event of an accident. Take multiple photos of the following as evidence:

1. Vehicle damage
2. Property damage
3. Skid marks, debris, vehicle positions, and road conditions
4. Location markers: intersections, addresses, exit numbers, etc.
5. Identification cards of all involved
6. Insurance cards of all involved

This information is meant to help gain a better understanding of what should be recorded in the case of an automobile accident. Please be responsible and refrain from any distracting activities while driving. Texting, phone calls, and road head can wait.

IV. How to Jump a Vehicle

First off, I should state that this information pertains to jumping your vehicle with the use of cables and another vehicle, not by rolling your car down a hill with the intent of manually starting it. I do not wish to endorse some fiery death where a car plummets off of a cliff and pancakes onto the ground all because they used some rolling technique to get their vehicle started. That being said, let's get to it.

Step 1: Gather your tools. First off, you will need jumper cables, a working vehicle, and some gloves for protection. Park the working vehicle directly in front of the vehicle in need of a jump start so that their front bumpers are facing one another.

Step 2: Shut off your vehicle and electronics. Ensure both vehicles and their radios are turned off. Open up the battery compartment on both vehicles in order to expose the batteries. You will notice that both batteries have a positive (+) and negative (-) terminal. Wearing gloves, take any protective covers off of the terminals and you're ready to go.

Step 3: Unwind the jumper cables for safety purposes. Once the cables are connected to a battery, you must make sure that the red and black ends never touch one another. This can cause arcing and/or damage to the vehicles.

Step 4: Get ready to jump. Connect the jumper cables in the following order:

1. Connect a single red clamp to the positive (+) terminal located on the dead battery.
2. Connect the other red clamp to the positive (+) terminal located on the working battery.

3. Connect a single black clamp to the negative (-) terminal of the working battery.
4. Connect the other black clamp to a piece of grounded metal on the dead car. One such location that should be suitable involves the bolt where the negative cable from the battery connects to the chassis (otherwise known as the main supporting structure of the vehicle).

Step 5: Double check the cables. Before turning on the vehicles, make sure that the jumper cables aren't tangled up inside the engine. There are many moving parts within a vehicle's engine, and the last thing you want are your cables to get caught up in the action.

Step 6: Start the working vehicle. Let the vehicle idle for about a minute or so. This will give it time to charge the dead battery of the other vehicle.

Step 7: Start the dead vehicle. If it does not start, ensure that the clamps are connected to their respective terminals and that the connections are secure. A slight wiggle or twist may be needed to increase the flow between cables.

Step 8: Remove the cables. If the dead vehicle starts, prevent short circuiting by removing the jumper cables in the opposite order in which you attached them.

1. Disconnect the black clamp from the negative (-) terminal (grounded metal) located on the car with the previously dead battery.
2. Disconnect the black clamp from the negative (-) terminal located on the good battery.
3. Disconnect the red clamp from the positive (+) terminal located on the good battery.
4. Disconnect the red clamp from the positive (+) terminal located on the previously dead battery.

Step 9: Recharge your battery. Apply the protective covers to the batteries and close the hoods while keeping the dead vehicle running. Let it sit for about five to ten minutes to let the battery recharge.

Note: If the car fails to start with the use of cables or shortly after a successful jump, you may have a completely dead battery. In that case, refer to the section entitled, "How to Change a Car Battery" found earlier in this chapter.

V. How to Parallel Park

This one is for the ladies (just kidding, but not really). There is this notion that parallel parking is some frighteningly difficult task that only wizards and magicians can seem to perform. In reality, it is as easy or as difficult as you make it depending on your approach.

Step 1: Identify a parking spot. Find a suitable space large enough to fit your vehicle and then some - you don't want to be that asshole that goes bumper to bumper with the surrounding vehicles.

Step 2: Pull up next to the vehicle in front of the open spot. You never want to pull into a parallel parking spot head first. Being that most vehicles utilize their front wheels for steering, reversing into a parallel parking spot is much easier than diving on in. By pulling up next to the front car, you're allowing yourself to back up easily. Be sure to turn on your blinker to alert incoming cars that you'll be making an attempt to park.

Step 3: Back it up. Put your car in reverse and crank that wheel to the right to start backing in (image on next page). You'll want to come in at a rather sharp angle in the beginning in order to get as close to the curb as possible. Keep backing in until your front bumper slightly passes by the front car's rear bumper.

Step 4: Get parallel to the curb. Once you are clear of the front car's rear bumper, crank your wheel to the left in order to start straightening out your vehicle. Keep in mind that you're still in reverse, so keep a close eye on the car behind you. Once you've completed this maneuver, the rear end of your car should be rather close to both the curb and the car behind you.

Step 5: Straighten out your vehicle. Crank your wheel back to the right and inch forward to straighten out. Once this has been completed, you should be firmly planted in the parallel parking spot. To be courteous, center your car to give the other vehicles equal space both in front of and behind you.

Note: If you happen to kiss the curb while performing this process, simply pull back out and try again because, after all, shit happens. Ensure that you are using your blinkers and mirrors to avoid any collisions while performing this maneuver. If you happen to scrape another vehicle, refer to section III of this chapter entitled, "How to Gather Information in the Case of an Accident."

VI. How to Put on Snow Chains

For those of you that have absolutely no need for snow chains because you live in sunny San Diego or some other paradise, feel free to skip this section. Otherwise, carry on.

Step 1: Know the dimensions of your tires as well as the drive train of your vehicle. The dimensions can be found along the outside of your tire, just above the hub cap or rim. You will need these dimensions when purchasing your chains. With regard to your drive train, if your vehicle is front wheel drive, you only need chains on your front two tires. If your vehicle is four wheel or all wheel drive, it is recommended that you put chains on all tires.

Step 2: Find a flat surface to apply the snow chains to your tires. Performing this on a mountain side while driving uphill could easily become a recipe for disaster.

Step 3: Untangle the chains so that there are no kinks. It should naturally form a web-like shape. Once untangled, lay the chain down and ensure that any traction bars (if applicable) are facing away from the tire as they are here to grip the road.

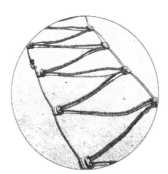

Step 4: Drape the chain over the top of your tire. Again, if your chains have traction bars, ensure that they are facing up and away from the tire itself. Cover the three-quarters of the tire that are not touching the ground while ensuring that the chain is running evenly along the tread. Tuck any excess chain under the tire to prep for step 5. If needed, a visual has been provided on the next page.

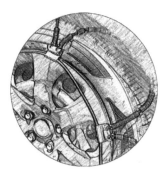

Step 5: Completely connect the chains. Pull your vehicle forward just enough to uncover the excess chain that has yet to be wrapped around your tire. Once completed, connect the chain ends together so that now, the chain is completely and evenly wrapped around your tire. Start by connecting the inner chain and work your way to the outside.

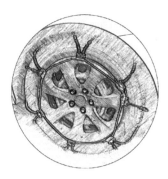

Step 6: Tighten your chains. Traditional chains will come with a d-cam tightening tool, a device used to aid in the tightening of your chains. Use the tool to make sure your chains are firmly hugging your tire.

Step 7: Rinse and repeat. Repeat this process with all other necessary tires. When completed, double check that your chains are snug and take your vehicle for a short, quarter-mile test drive.

Step 8: Tighten once more. Stop the vehicle after a brief drive and re-tighten your chains. You don't want them slipping off just before hitting a patch of black ice.

2
CLOTHING ADVICE

I. How to Do Your Laundry

Washing clothes is a pain in the ass, especially for men who have had their mothers wash their cum socks since they could shoot a load. It's time to grow the fuck up and do your own laundry, and that doesn't mean throwing everything you own into one load. If you would like a non-detailed version of how to wash clothes, there is a condensed step-by-step list at the end of this section.

Step 1: Sort your clothing. Clothes should be sorted into three categories: whites, light colors, and dark colors. Don't be a dipshit; whites are pretty self-explanatory. Light colors traditionally include your light blues, grays, yellows, etc. Dark colors, on the other hand, are usually made up of blacks, reds, blues, or dark greens.

Step 2: Empty your pockets. Once your clothes are sorted, the next step is to take everything out of the pockets. Sharp objects will slice your clothes so make sure you take them out.

Step 3: Prepare to remove your stains. Next up comes removing shart stains. This is where stain remover comes in handy. Stain removers can vary, so the product's instructions will tell you how it

GROW THE F*CK UP

should be applied. If you happen to be washing denim, be sure to spray it for stains and turn it inside out to prevent the color from fading. For buttoned apparel, fully button any shirts, give them a good spray or two, and turn them inside out as well to prevent them from catching and tearing during the washing and drying cycles.

Step 4: It's time to wash. If you must use bleach, please don't use it on colored clothes. If you use bleach on colored clothing, it'll most likely be destroyed. The next step is to add detergent. This is added to all loads. Your specific type of detergent will tell you how much solution to add as well as what it smells like if you happen to care. Don't think you're fucking Einstein by adding twice the recommended amount. You'd just end up wasting detergent while making your clothes slosh around in a sudsy hell.

Step 5: Set your temperature settings. Now that you are ready to start the wash, you need to set your washer to the correct temperature. I generally wash all of my colored clothes on cold to prevent them from shrinking. Whites can be washed in either warm or cold water, however I recommend cold to prevent them from shrinking as well. As a side note, you dirty, sweaty fucks with soggy sheets can wash your bed linens and pillowcases in hot water to kill those nasty ass germs.

Step 6: It's time to dry. Once the clothes have been through the wash, empty the lint tray in the dryer and toss your wet load inside. Insert a dryer sheet to prevent static build-up, set the dryer to the correct temperature, and start it up. Once the clothes have finished their cycle, simply fold them or throw them in the closet as many of you dirty bastards do. That's all there is to it.

For you simple folk who refuse to read and want a shortcut on washing your clothes, I have compiled a brief list of steps below.

Step 1: Sort clothes into whites, light colors, and dark colors.

Step 2: Dig through your pockets to make sure nothing important gets washed by accident.

Step 3: Apply stain remover to clothing and turn buttoned/denim apparel inside out. Make sure that buttoned apparel is fully buttoned prior to washing.

Step 4: Put clothes in the washer and add detergent. Only add bleach to whites.

Step 5: Wash whites on either cold or warm. Wash lights and darks on cold. Cold water prevents clothing from shrinking. Pillowcases and bed sheets can be washed on hot to kill germs.

Step 6: Empty the lint tray in the dryer and transfer your clothes from the washer to the dryer. Throw in a dryer sheet to prevent static build-up. Dry on the appropriate heat setting.

Step 7: Do with your dry clothes as you wish.

II. How to Fold a Shirt

This one should be a no-brainer; however, I will briefly outline how to fold a shirt properly:

Step 1: Prepare to fold. Lay your button up or flamboyant v-neck face down and smooth it out. It should be wrinkle free like an 80-year-old after a gallon of Botox.

Step 2: Make your first fold. Take either side of the shirt and fold it inward about 1/3 of the way.

Step 3: Fold downward. Take the sleeve of the just-folded side and fold it neatly downwards toward the bottom of the shirt. The sleeve should align with the side of the shirt. This one may be difficult to envision, therefore I have depicted this step at the top of the next page.

Step 4: Rinse and repeat. Same folds, other side. Bam.

Step 5: Tackling the tail. Fold the shirt tail upward about six inches or so.

Step 6: Double it up. Fold the bottom half of the shirt once more so that the bottom just brushes against the collar (image on next page).

Step 7: Reveal your masterpiece. Flip the shirt over and you should have yourself a nicely folded piece of clothing.

If you would like to learn other ways to keep your clothes looking fresh, you'll have to wait for the deluxe version of this book (which may never happen).

III. How to Iron Your Clothes

All clothes shouldn't be ironed in the same manner. Therefore, I have created a how-to for shirts and pants below.

When ironing, keep in mind that the wrong heat setting can ruin an article of clothing. Cotton can be ironed on high. Wool and rayon fabrics should be ironed on medium. Finally, silk and polyester should be ironed on low. When it comes to these low-setting fabrics, it is also advised that you use a linen barrier or baking paper in between the iron and fabric to prevent burns.

Now before you begin, you should have the necessary equipment to effectively iron your clothing. You'll need an iron, an ironing board, and some distilled water for the iron itself.

Shirts:

Step 1: Preparation. Pour some distilled water in the allotted compartment on the iron, check to see what fabric your clothing is made of, and set the iron's temperature to the appropriate setting. This information will be located on your clothing tag. Tags can generally be found either in the collar or down in the body of your shirt along the seam.

Step 2: Tackle the sleeves. As seen on the next page, you'll want to iron the sleeves first to prevent wrinkling the body of the shirt later on. Keep the iron moving at all times to avoid burning your fabric.

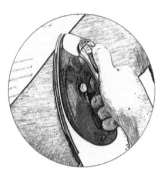

Step 3: Work the body. Put the shirt on the ironing board and work those magical hands of yours. Start with the larger areas and work your way to the edges of the shirt.

Step 4: Gently remove your top. Pull the shirt away from you when taking it off the ironing board. If you yank the shirt towards you, it may cause it to wrinkle once again.

Step 5: Put it away nicely. Hang your shirt when you are done or fold it properly to avoid a wrinkled mess. You took the time to iron the fucking thing, so take a few seconds to put it away correctly.

Pants:

Step 1: Lay em' down. Don't make this harder than it is. Lay one pant leg down flat with one seam on the left and one on the right. Feel free to let the other leg drape down toward the floor while it waits its turn.

Step 2: Go down the middle. Iron straight down the middle to avoid fucking anything up.

Step 3: Same thing, other side. Repeat the process with the other leg and you're done.

Pleated Pants:

Step 1: Match the seams. Lay the pants down flat, but this time with the seems matching up with one another in the middle. The seams should be running straight down the middle of the legs rather than on the sides.

Step 2: Iron straight down the middle. Ensure that you keep the seams matched up with one another. You want the pleat to run straight up and down the front and back of your pants, not toward your moose knuckle.

Step 3: Repeat. Iron the other leg and you're good to go.

IV. How to Sew a Decent Button

Odds are you probably sew a pretty crappy button. That's about to change. Below you will find a concoction of sewing techniques that will allow you to sew a button like a kid in a sweat shop.

Step 1: Grab the necessary tools. Unless you can use your pecker as a needle, you are going to need some tools. Grab a sewing kit with the following: thread, a needle (or two), a button, and scissors.

Step 2: Thread the needle with about two feet of thread. This shouldn't be all that difficult. Pull the thread half way through the needle and tie the ends together to double up the string.

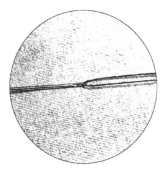

Step 3: Get your button in place. Now that you have prepped the needle and string, place the button in the desired location. Stick the needle through the back of your article of clothing and through one of the holes in the button.

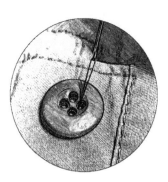

Step 4: Set your spacer. Lay another needle (or toothpick if necessary) flat on top of the button and in-between the holes that you will be threading. This will be used as a spacer.

Step 5: Time to thread. Bring the threaded needle *over* the spacer and through the next hole.

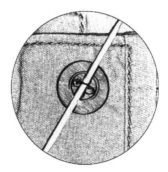

Step 6: Thread and thread again. Repeat steps three through five a few times with all available button holes. Feel free to double or triple patterns that have already been used. Finish with the needle going through the back and out the front to prep for the final steps.

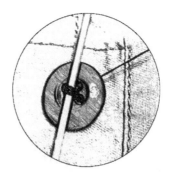

Step 7: Remove the spacer. Using the threaded needle, wrap the base of the button and thread it through to the back once more, but this time without going through a button hole. If you're having a hard time imagining this step, feel free to check out the image at the top of the next page.

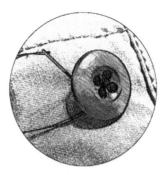

Step 8: Finish it off. Take the threaded needle and tie a knot. If you can tie your shoes, you should be able to accomplish this step. Cut the needle away from the thread and you're good to go.

V. How to Tie a Tie

If you use a clip-on tie, you probably tuck your penis between your legs. This lesson is here to restore your testicles. Illustrations are provided for each step to make it as easy as possible to understand. Before we begin, I should state that there are a few different ways to tie a tie. This lesson pertains to the four-in-hand style.

Step 1: Bring the tie around your neck. Have the wide side in your dominant hand and the thin side in the other. Pull the wide side until the bottom of that end touches your pecker.

Step 2: Cross em' over. Bring the wide end of the tie in front of the thin end. Perform this step at about nipple height. If you don't like my nipple recommendation, some people wrap it around the seam on the thin side. This generally makes my tie too long, but do as you wish.

Step 3: Bring it back now. Bring the wide end of the tie behind the thin end. This will cause a sort of fold over the thin end itself.

Step 4: Fold the wide end of the tie once more. This time however, go around the front. You will be creating a knot of sorts which will be used in the next few steps.

Step 5: Bring it under. You will now bring the wide end of the tie under the loop around your neck.

Step 6: Whip it out. Take the wide end and, with it facing forward, pull it through the front of the knot that has been created through previous steps.

Step 7: Make it snug. With the wide end pulled down as far as possible, slide the knot up along the thin side to tighten the tie around your neck.

Step 8: Go flaunt your tie you sexy beast. Make sure the knot is snug against your collar and tuck the thin end of the tie neatly into its holster. Once you're ready to take it off, feel free to use it to tie a loved one to the bed post.

VI. How to Wear a Suit

This section is more or less a mesh of what to do and what not to do when wearing a suit. By choosing the right suit, you can not only look professional, but you can also look damn good for the ladies.

Step 1: Find a professional. Unless you're an expert on your dimensions, go see a tailor. They can set you up with a suit that will hug your body without constricting your movement. On the other hand, if you want to look unprofessional, you're more than welcome to go buy a suit from your local thrift shop.

Step 2: Customization is key. Purchase a suit that has yet to be hemmed. This will allow you to essentially create a suit that was made for your... "unique" body.

Step 3: Grab a nice top. Choose a dress shirt and throw on your suit. Your dress shirt should be a long sleeved, collared button up without pockets. You want to stand out without looking overly flamboyant, so avoid neon colored shirts. A simple white, gray, or blue shirt should do the trick.

Step 4: Show off those cuffs. When wearing your jacket, your dress shirt cuffs and collar should be exposed by about a half inch or so. The tail of the jacket should barely cover the top of your bum.

Step 5: Button it right. When buttoning your jacket, never button the bottom button. When you go to sit down, unbutton your jacket altogether to keep it from wearing out the button and riding up.

Step 6: Don't sag. Make sure your pants are at your waist. They should fit so that you have enough room around the crotch so it doesn't feel constricting (trust me, no one wants to see your moose knuckle).

Step 7: Get em' hemmed. Hem your pants so that they sit nicely on top of your shoes and just above the heel. Again, go to a tailor to have this done. They will adjust your pants appropriately.

Step 8: Buy some professional accessories. You will want a nice tie, belt, dress socks, and a pair of shoes. If you're feeling fashionable, grab a nice watch as well.

Step 9: Match your accessories. Your shoes and belt should match one another and your socks should match your pants. I feel as though this is pretty self-explanatory, so don't fuck it up.

Step 10: Look fly with a tie. Choose a tie that complements your shirt and suit combination.

Step 11: Check yourself out. Put it all together and you're good to go. Go land that big boy job you've been dreaming of.

3

EMPLOYMENT ADVICE

I. How to Create a Resume and Cover Letter

This will not be a detailed description on how to write every resume and cover letter known to man. Instead, it will outline key points that should be utilized in both documents.

When creating a cover letter:

Tip 1: Keep it short. You're not writing a manifesto. Your cover letter should be about a half a page in length. Any shorter and you may lose credibility, but any longer and it may not get read at all.

Tip 2: Leave out details from your resume. Your cover letter is not meant to be a summary of your resume; plain and simple. The person evaluating your resume can fucking read, so don't make them read the same thing twice - that's absurd and redundant. Instead, add something unique that gives the reader some insight into who you are, what you're passionate about, what your story is, etc. Finally, be sure to sound sane. No one needs to read about how you like to walk around in lace panties and stick your dick in chocolate cake on the weekends.

Pieces of a cover letter:

Part 1: A catchy opening line. If you know someone within the company that recommended you apply for a position, throw that out there. You want something that makes you stand out from the other hundreds of applicants. If you are not fortunate enough to know someone internally, be unique. Use anecdotes or story telling to pique the reader's interest.

Part 2: Show interest and expertise in the body. The body of your cover letter should show that you want to work for said employer. Some background knowledge of the company's industry could help in this instance. You also need to explain why you are qualified for the position. For example, if a company needs a financial analyst and you think the square root of 81 is potato, you are fucked.

Part 3: Make your closing sentence clear and concise. Finish off with a brief explanation (and I do mean brief) of how your experience makes you the best candidate for the position and be sure to thank them for their time. If you are told that the employer will be in touch with you, wait patiently for a response. If nothing was stated, simply let them know how and when you will be in touch.

When creating a resume:

Tip 1: The main points. There are generally four main sections: Contact information, education, experience, and additional data.

Tip 2: Keep the format simple. There are dozens of ways to format a resume. Do not go with a complex format that is difficult to follow. A reader should be able to easily follow the information detailed in all sections of your resume.

The sections of a resume:

Part 1: Contact information. At a minimum, you will want to include your full name, e-mail address, permanent home address, and phone number. If you own a fax machine in this millennia, please refrain from including it in your information. Right after that, do us all a favor and throw that piece of shit off a cliff.

Part 2: Education. If you are fortunate enough to have obtained a college degree, simply state where you went to school, what your degree was in, and what year you graduated. If you are currently pursuing higher education, throw that in there. If not, simply state where you went to high school and what year you graduated.

Part 3: Experience. Starting with your most recent work, you will want to list all relevant experience and dates of employment whether it be professional, volunteer, field work, or other. You will want to highlight what you did in each instance. Personally, I use around three bullet points that touch on my responsibilities, accomplishments, and involvement in each scenario. Again, put them in chronological order starting out with your most recent experience. This will make it easier for the reader to follow your job history.

Part 4: Additional data. Here you will want to include honors and skills not mentioned in the experience section. For instance, let's say you gobbled the knob of every teacher in college causing you to graduate magna cum laude. Throw that accomplishment in this section (your academic accomplishment, not your ability to suck like a vacuum). You may also want to add proficiencies and interests. Letting the employer know you're proficient in Excel and other software applications can prove very useful. Interests, on the other hand, can help to make a more personal connection with your employer. A past professor once stated that he was chosen among other applicants because he stated that football was one of his interests.

That is really all there is to it. Essentially you are only going to have to strain your brain when it comes to the cover letter and even then, it is only half a page of material. Other than that, the rest is basically a summary of your life's work academically and professionally up till now. Best of luck!

II. How to Prepare for a Job Interview

Job interviews can be stressful, however much of the stress is unnecessarily created by the interviewee prior to the big day. The outline below touches on ways that you can become more prepared for a job interview so you don't sweat through your business attire and smell like shit before you can say, "hello."

Step 1: Do your homework. Days before your interview, do some research on the company that you will be interviewing with. Nothing gives a manager a bigger boner than you having accurate background knowledge on their company. When I say accurate, I mean that anything can be posted online so it is important to verify and ensure that your information is coming from a credible source (company website, scholarly research articles, and other things of that nature). Doing your research shows that you are not only serious about this opportunity, but that you are professional as well.

Step 2: Choose your wardrobe ahead of time. If you traditionally interview in jeans and a t-shirt, it's time to grow the fuck up. Dress like a true professional. For you men, wear a suit and tie with a nice collared shirt underneath. Ladies, wear a formal skirt with a suit jacket or a conservative dress. Whatever the case, dress in formal, professional attire. Your clothes make the first impression, so choose them carefully ahead of time.

Step 3: Know your strengths and weaknesses. I can almost guarantee that you will be asked what your strengths and weaknesses are. Don't give some bullshit answer like, "I don't have any weaknesses" or, "I believe that everyone has something they could improve on because no one is perfect." You're not impressing anyone with that answer and you will simply look like an imbecile. Put some thought into this and really dig into what your strengths and weaknesses are and have examples for each. For instance, maybe your organizational skills are impeccable and you have the ability to prioritize in a fast-paced environment. On the other hand, you could be terrible at speaking in front of groups or demanding more out of others in a constructive way. Regardless, know your strengths and weaknesses and be able to speak to them.

Step 4: Formulate your own questions ahead of time. I have asked interviewees time and time again if they have questions for me. Approximately 90% of them reply with a resounding no. Asking questions not only shows that you're interested, but that you have the capacity to think for yourself.

Step 5: Plan to leave early for the interview. I hate nothing more than people who fail to show up on time. It is not only a sure way to fail a job interview, but it is also disrespectful to the interviewer. Plan to arrive at least fifteen minutes early to your interview. If you're anticipating traffic, leave even earlier. Do not be late under any circumstances. If you're late, you had better come up with a damn good excuse such as, "my car wouldn't start because the breathalyzer said I was intoxicated."

All in all, job interviews are as easy or as difficult as you make them. If you follow the points listed above, it will simply make the interview process a little smoother while hopefully increasing the odds of you landing a job.

III. How to Write a Proper Email

While many people make writing an email a daunting task, writing a proper email is simple. There are a few key parts that need to be included to make it look prim and proper. Those parts have been outlined below:

Step 1: Use a professional email address. Your email address shouldn't resemble your gamer tag. Instead, choose something formal that resembles your real name. This not only comes off in a more professional manner, but it is easier for the receiver to identify who the sender of an email is.

Step 2: Keep the subject line short and sweet. The body of your email can explain the subject, so keep the subject line of the email short and to the point. For example, if you're sending out a memo for December 3rd that contains a plethora of information, you could simply entitle the email, "Memo 12/3" or something of the sort. There is no need for excessive detail in this section.

Step 3: Start the email with a proper salutation. Kick off your email with a simple, "Dear *(insert person's name here)*," and be sure to address them by their last name. If you don't know the person you're about to email, addressing them by first name will just make you look like a cocky prick. Be cordial while keeping it short and sweet.

Example: Dear Mr. Smith,

Step 4: Use proper grammar and punctuation in the body of the email. You're not texting a friend or for that matter, texting at all. If your emails are similar to the messages on your phone, you're probably the reason warning labels are created. Emails should contain proper spelling and punctuation while addressing the subject that was, you guessed it, written in none other than the subject line.

Step 5: Use a proper complementary close. Once your body paragraph is all said and done, you're good to close out the email with a valediction of your choosing. Personally, I use "Sincerely," as it can be used in virtually every instance, followed by my full name and contact information.

Example: Sincerely,
John Smith
(555)555-5555
John.Smith@email.com

Step 6: Proofread and send. Once you have all of the above completed, read over your email and use spell check. You're not a dictionary or a spelling savant, so take the two seconds to click the fucking button that literally checks your spelling for you. When all looks good, hit send.

Being that email is a primary form of communication for many people in both personal and business settings, it is important to know how to write one in a proper manner. So please, take the time to write a well thought out email with all of the necessary information.

4

FINANCIAL ADVICE

I. How to Apply for College Loans

We may as well have dildos installed on all chairs in the classroom because when it comes to college tuition, we are getting fucked. Hard. That being said, there are many avenues available when it comes to applying for college loans. Much of the information surrounding the application itself will vary based on which avenue you choose; therefore, I have outlined three main options below that give students the opportunity to take out a loan or gain monetary assistance when going to college.

Step 1: Start with the FAFSA/federal loans. The Free Application for Federal Student Aid is essentially the mother of applications that must be completed in order to obtain any sort of Federal financial aid. To start your application, simply go online to fafsa.ed.gov and follow the links. When completed, you'll basically be put into contention for federal grants, work-study programs, loans, and in some cases, state aid as well. If you're white and middle class, good luck getting a grant, but be sure to fill out the application regardless. If you're any other ethnicity, fill that bitch out and thank those lovely taxpayers for the dozens of 30-packs you'll most likely be buying with their tax dollars.

Step 2: Look into student loan providers. Under this umbrella we can find companies that essentially give you a loan in return for interest and principal payments from you, the borrower. These companies also handle billing and other services related to your loans. If you've applied for the FAFSA and didn't receive a cent, this may be a route to take.

Step 3: Look into retail banks. These are comprised of your general banks and other various financial institutions. The services are similar to that of any other lender and in some cases, private institutions will charge you a fee for document handling and other various services. There are some banks that will waive this fee if you are a student.

All in all, choosing a lender can be a daunting task. I would personally start with completing the FAFSA because it essentially covers all your bases for a federal loan while making you eligible for grants. If that avenue proves to be unsuccessful, then I would recommend looking to either a retail bank or student loan provider. Best of luck and use a condom.

II. How to Apply for and Use a Credit Card

Before I even broach this subject, I should make it clear that applying for and being approved for a credit card does not mean that you all of a sudden have this never-before-seen influx of free money. Just because you may qualify for a ten thousand dollar credit limit does not mean you have ten thousand dollars to spend. Do that and you will have what we American's like to call debt (otherwise known as money you never really had and decided to spend anyways). That being said, the application process and insight on how to use a credit card has been outlined below.

Applying for a credit card:

Step 1: Get your finances in order. No bank in their right mind is going to give a credit card to a customer with overdue loans, late housing payments, etc. Once you're financially stable, you may want to look into a credit card.

Step 2: Find a steady job. While easier said than done, a job will give you a little more leeway when applying for a credit card. If you're under 21, the law requires customers in the application process to have a steady flow of income (otherwise known as verifiable income) before they can be approved for a credit card. If you are unable to secure a steady job at the moment, you may need someone to cosign for you.

Step 3: Don't go ape shit with applications. Each application initiated by you, the customer, takes a toll on your credit score. Therefore, it is not wise to apply for multiple credit cards at once. If your applications are declined, you're not only shit out of luck, but you've tanked your credit score as well. Now if the bank has gone ahead and pre-approved you without your knowledge, your score won't be affected. Just be aware that some credit cards come with an annual fee ranging anywhere from $25 to $100, so you may want to stay away from these cards when starting to build credit.

Step 4: Try your hand at an application. If you have a checking account or savings account with a specific bank and you've been responsible with that account, try applying for a credit card with them first. Your history may prove to be beneficial in this instance. If that fails, shoot for a retail establishment or department store. These credit cards are generally easier to qualify for; however they tend to have higher monthly interest rates. Finally, if you're a student, many banks offer student credit cards that are easy to be approved for. However, much like retail establishments, these cards tend to have higher monthly interest rates.

Step 5: Read the terms of your agreement. You always want to read the terms of your agreement before signing up for a credit card otherwise you may end up getting screwed with no lube. Some things you'll want to look at are interest rates, associated fees, and rewards associated with a particular card.

How to use a credit card:

Step 1: Start small and pay off debts in a timely manner. When you receive your first credit card, the object is not to cap out your limit on day one. Instead, use it sparingly. By doing so, you'll be establishing credit while racking up manageable expenses that should be easy to pay off.

Step 2: Do not spend more than you have. For example, if you have $5,000 in the bank and you just put $10,000 worth of sex toys and male enhancement pills on your credit card, you single handedly just incurred debt that you probably won't be able to pay back any time soon. Your debt will then start to accrue interest and continue to get worse when you miss your payment deadlines. Take the following example for instance: You have a balance of $5,000. With a minimum payment of 100 dollars a month at an interest rate of 19.9%, it will take 109 months (approximately nine years) to pay off the debt. By that time, you will have paid an additional $5,852 in interest all because you spent money you simply didn't have.

Step 3: Pay off your debts in full. Sure, paying the minimum that you owe each month sounds nice until you end up paying interest for your debt. It will make your life much easier if you pay off all of your debt at once. You won't have to worry about interest fees or rolling debt. Instead, you'll be building your credit score in a constructive manner.

Step 4: Review your credit card statements. Each month you will be sent a statement from your credit card provider. If you have internet, get a paperless statement to help out the environment. Once you get your statement, look it over. Plain and simple. Humans fuck up from time to time, so odds are you will catch a mistake once in a while. Don't only look for accuracy, but look for fraudulent charges as well. I literally checked my balance one morning while dropping a deuce. Needless to say, some bastard in Illinois used my credit card an hour earlier to buy a movie. Learn from me and check your account activity.

III. How to Buy a Car

So, you want to purchase a vehicle but you're unsure how to go about it? That is quite alright. The outline below will give you insight on what you can do prior to and during the purchase of a vehicle. Keep in mind that if you want a new vehicle, the value of your vehicle will plummet once it is purchased and driven off the lot. Although it may not have the features or new car smell that will make you cream in your jeans, you may find a used car to be of better value.

Step 1: Know what you want in a car. Sure, a vibrating seat and cock massager sound like they would be nice additions while driving, but are they necessary? Write down what you would like such as auxiliary ports, wireless capabilities, safety specs, and other things of that nature. Be willing to give or take because your dream car will most likely cost you an arm and a leg.

Step 2: Set a budget. Know what you are and are not willing to pay when walking onto a lot. Most car dealers are sharks looking to get the highest price for their goods because their pay is commission based.

Step 3: Take your budget and your wants, mesh them together, and do some more research. At this point, you should be able to find a car that matches your needs. However, if a new car tickles your fancy, know this: The general rule of thumb is that a vehicle loses 9% of its value immediately after it leaves the dealership lot. In one year, it loses 19% of the value. At five years, 60%. Basically, a new $20,000 car will be worth around $8,000 dollars only a few years down the road. Is new the way to go? That's up to you.

Step 4: Shop around and see what you can find. No two dealerships tend to be the same, so be sure to take the time to visit a few. When browsing, don't go in with the mentality that you're going to drive off the lot in a new ride. Simply window shop.

Step 5: Find the invoice price of the car that you are looking at. This price will represent what the dealer paid for the vehicle itself. By arming yourself with this tool, it will allow you to be in a better bargaining position later on when you go to purchase the vehicle.

Step 6: Have your finances in check before showing interest in purchasing a vehicle. A good start is to know your credit score. You can obtain this information once a year from a major credit reporting agency. If your score is in the dump, take some time to pay off your debt and get your score to where it should be. This will enable you to receive lower interest rates as well as a potential loan.

Step 7: Get ready to bargain. In a car buying scenario, both the dealer and buyer are looking to get the best deal. If you have all available information about the vehicle you are looking to purchase, you've put yourself in a good position. However, no matter how good that position may be, always be prepared to walk away. After all, the income of a dealership is derived from selling cars. Without you signing the paperwork for some keys at the end of the day, they are shit out of luck. Ultimately you have the upper hand, so don't get guilted or scammed into paying more than you have to for a vehicle, especially when dealers try to sweeten the deal through services and perks. Instead, drive a hard bargain.

IV. How to Complete Your Taxes

Hire a qualified tax accountant. Plain and simple. If you're reading this book, it's probably because someone in your life has found that you lack the ability to accomplish the most basic of tasks in life. Because you may be prone to missing important information that would need to be included in your tax forms, odds are you will botch your chances of getting a half way decent tax return on your own. Therefore, I have taken the strain out of your brain by telling you plain and simple: Hire a qualified professional to prepare your fucking taxes.

V. How to Find and Use Coupons

But only people with tight assholes use coupons, right? If that's the case, then you're going to need a gallon of lube to tickle my prostate. That dollar bill in your wallet is made of the same material as a coupon minus the cotton. It also probably has the remnants of a coked out hooker who has had one too many abortions, but we won't worry about that. What we will focus on is the fact that both objects hold monetary value.

Coupons can be found in a variety of places. If you're wanting a physical coupon, search in the following places:

1. In your local Sunday newspaper
2. On the back of receipts
3. On product packages
4. Inside magazines

Electronic coupons are another, more abundant form of coupons. These can be found on:

1. Coupon websites
2. Retail establishment websites
3. Manufacturer websites
4. Mobile applications
5. Social media sites

Once you have found an enticing coupon, it is important to note that it most likely has an expiration date, therefore be sure to use it while it is valid. Other than that, using it is as simple as handing it to the person who will be ringing you up when all is said and done. For example, if you are going out to dinner, you will want to hand the coupon to your waiter. Sure, handing a coupon to a waiter while taking your significant other out to dinner may make you look cheap, but in the end, they are eating for free so they can shove their opinions up their rectum.

VI. How to Manage Your Money

Managing money is not a difficult thing to do. Much of it comes down to knowing what your income and expenses amount to over time, thus allowing you to gradually save your cash or invest in the future. Below you will find a three step plan to managing your money in a more effective manner.

Step 1: Know your monthly income. How can you determine what you can and cannot buy if you have no clue how much money you are bringing in? You simply cannot. The first step in managing your money is knowing your income or rather, how much money you bring in over a period of time. Start writing down your income to know what you'll be working with from here on out.

Step 2: Know your expenses. Write down everything you purchase over the course of a month. This includes everything from groceries to gas, clothing, entertainment, food, the morning after pill, and more. Once you have totaled all of your expenses over the course of a month, determine how much you have left from your overall income. If you are spending more than you make, you are accruing debt. If your car is worth more than your home, you probably fucked yourself there too. In these cases, you will probably need to cut some non-essential expenses to make ends meet. However, if you happen to have some cash left over, you are in good standing. Find a way to save or invest that money in your future to set yourself up for retirement.

Step 3: Cut out the non-essentials. Do you get your hair cut by a professional and purchase clothing from brand name designers? Are you eating dinner that costs a day's worth of pay? While it may make you more popular among your peers, it's most likely impacting your budget. Purchase a hair cutting kit and do it yourself, meal prep every now and then, or buy clothing without a brand name on the front. Clothing is made with the same material by the same kids in China - you are simply paying for the name. If you are struggling to make ends meet, simply find a way to cut out these non-essentials.

While the three step plan is nearly as simplistic as it gets, it will allow you to hopefully gain a better idea of what you can and cannot afford. Grasp these basics first, and then start to build a spreadsheet containing income and expenses. This will allow you to track your cash over a period of time while having everything in one place. Be mindful of how much you make and what you spend your hard earned money on. In other words, don't go buy a $70 pocket pussy when your hand can get the job done for free.

VII. How to Understand a 401k

If you're like a majority of the population, at one point you had no clue what the fuck a 401k was. To simplify it for you, a 401k is essentially a retirement savings plan for those employed by for-profit companies. In other words, it is a defined-contribution pension plan.

How it works: If you work for a for-profit company, odds are you have the option to invest in a 401k. You will choose how much of your paycheck to contribute to this pension plan. Traditionally, employees put in a percentage of their total paychecks as most companies will match your contribution up to a certain amount. The money is then used to invest in a variety of options such as stocks, bonds, money market investments, mutual funds, and more. Keep in mind there is a limit to how much you can invest in a 401k per year. You can typically find this information by visiting www.irs.gov.

Now, when you choose to invest in a 401k, the money invested comes out of your paycheck prior to being taxed. Because you can't evade taxes, AKA tax evasion, you will be taxed on your 401k savings when you choose to withdraw it from your account decades down the line.

You choose your investments: With a 401k, you can choose to invest your money in a variety of ways. Create your own portfolio of stocks and bonds or invest in portfolios that have been pre-set by your employer. The rule of thumb is that you want to start out extremely risky and then gradually lower your risk over time as you near retirement. Keep in mind that more risk can have great returns as well as great losses, so do your research before investing.

Caveats: In most cases, your employer will make you wait a certain amount of time before you can participate in a 401k. You may also have to put in a certain number of hours with the company before you can even gain access. Last but not least, there are usually rules that determine when you are eligible to withdraw money. If you withdraw before said date, there are usually penalty fees upon withdrawal.

All in all, that's really all there is to it. Is it wise to invest in a 401k? Absofuckinglutely. If your company is willing to match your contribution up to a certain percentage, max that shit out and invest wisely. The payoff years down the line can be astounding if you get in early.

VIII. How to Write a Check

Interestingly enough, when young adults attempt to write a check nowadays, they practically shit a brick. In order to alleviate this issue, the steps to writing a check have been outlined below.

Step 1: Grab a pen. Never fill out a check using a pencil as this will make your check an easy target for forgers and thieves.

Step 2: Fill in the date. Grab your check and write the date in the upper right-hand corner on the line marked "date." If the word "date" is not present, do not panic. Continue to write the date in that location.

Step 3: Pay to the order of.. Write the name of the recipient in the section marked "pay to" or "pay to the order of." If you are making a check out to a person, write in their name. If you are making the check out to a business, write the name of the business in this section. For example, pay to the order of ABC Company.

Step 4: Write the amount of the check next to the dollar sign.
The dollar sign is located on the right side of the check itself. Here you will input the numerical amount, such as $30.20. When writing in the amount, be sure to write it as close as possible to the dollar sign to prevent some sneaky shit from forging an extra digit.

Step 5: Spell out the amount. Write the amount of your check in word form. You will do this in the line located directly under the "pay to the order of" section. Be sure to include the cents when writing the amount so that someone else does not add more money to your check. If you're making out a check for fifty dollars, write "fifty and no/100." Once the amount has been written, draw a line running from the end of the word to the end of the line itself. This will prevent anyone from making out your check for more money.

Step 6: Sign your check. Your signature goes in the bottom right-hand corner. If you fail to sign the check, it will not be considered valid. Be sure to sign with the same signature to hopefully prevent possible forgeries in the future.

Step 7: Fill out the "memo" or "for" section. Located on the bottom left-hand side of a check, this section is where you can write what the check is for. While it is optional, it is useful in helping to remember why you paid something or what you paid it for. If you're writing a check as a gift, you could write "birthday." If it is for your monthly rent, you could put a brief description for that as well.

You are good to go. The check should be acceptable by any right-minded person or establishment so long as you can spell and count properly. If by chance you screwed something up, be sure to write "VOID" across the face of the check in large, bold letters. Finally, proceed to shred the check so that it can't be cashed by a thief in the future.

5

GRILLING ADVICE

I. How to Use a Charcoal Grill

Many people love the taste of meats cooked from a charcoal grill and now, so can you. Outlined below are the steps to using a charcoal grill like a manly man.

Step 1: Gather the essentials. You will need charcoal briquettes, charcoal lighter fluid, matches, and some tongs.

Step 2: Prepare the grill. Remove the grate, open the bottom vents, and clean out any ash or charred remains of your previous attempts at grilling. We are going to start off on a clean slate. Oh, and don't forget to mount the ash tray underneath the grill so it can catch the remnants of the coal. If you need to see this step in action, the correlating image can be found on the next page.

Step 3: Add some charcoal. Throw in your briquettes and pile them into a pyramid at the bottom of the grill. Spray them with a bit of charcoal lighter fluid, throw on a match, and let them burn.

Step 4: Let em' burn. Allow your briquettes to turn gray-ish white. Once this has occurred, they will be hot enough to do some mean grilling.

Step 5: Adjust the charcoal as needed. Spread the briquettes out based on what you are cooking. If you are cooking some thinner meats, you will probably want to spread the charcoal evenly across the bottom of the grill. If you are cooking thicker meats, then you will want to move the charcoal over to one side to let that shit sizzle while leaving a cooler pocket on the side with less charcoal. You can find a depiction of this step at the top of the next page.

Step 6: Prove your manliness. Put the grate on and cook away.

II. How to Use a Gas Grill

If you're looking for simplicity, a gas grill is the way to go. There's no fuss with charcoal and you can start it up with ease. While you'll be missing out on the smoky flavor, it just might tickle your fancy.

Step 1: Placement. Make sure that your grill is on a level surface and away from any flammable objects such as your home, furniture, and children. We don't need to burn shit down.

Step 2: Prep your fuel. Attach the propane tank and check for cracks or leaks in the gas line. One way to check is by lathering a soapy solution on the line. You will begin to see bubbles if there happens to be a leak while the gas is on. Also, you'll want to ensure that the control valve is shut tight.

Step 3: Light it up. Open the grill hood, open the propane control valve to allow the gas to flow, crank up the gas on the grill, and immediately press the ignition button (image on next page). The gas should ignite and you're ready to grill. If it does not light, wait several minutes and try it again as you do not want to light excessive amounts of propane gas through quick, successive attempts. Once the burners are lit, feel free to get grilling.

Step 4: Safely shut it down. When all is said and done, turn the burners and the propane control knob off. Personally, I like to clean my grill with a wire scrubber while it's still hot to prep for the next grilling session, but do as you wish.

III. How to Cook a Steak

Odds are you aren't a grill master, so I have outlined how to cook a steak on both a gas and charcoal grill. Now, there are a plethora of ways that one can go about grilling a savory slice of meat. If you disagree with the methods below, I couldn't really give a shit.

Steaks on a charcoal grill:

Step 1: Grab your manly grillin' tools. You will need some tongs, seasonings, charcoal, charcoal lighter fluid, a meat thermometer, and obviously some matches or a lighter.

Step 2: Throw on some charcoal. Pile the charcoal inside the grill in a pyramid-like manner, put a little lighter fluid on them, and light em' up. Be sure to close the lid and open the vents to allow for the charcoal to heat up and oxygen to flow on through. Once they turn a grey-ish white color, they are good to go. Move the charcoal to one side of the grill so that the charcoal side is hot like a MILF and the other side a bit cooler.

Step 3: Steak preparation. Let your steaks come up to room temperature, prep them with some seasoning, and place them on the grate of the grill. When prepping, you may also want to add some olive oil to the outside of the steaks in order to keep them from sticking to the grate of the grill. Once the steaks are ready to be set on the grate, throw them on and close the lid. Just keep your steaks away from open flames or you'll be eating charred remains.

Step 4: Refrain from touching your meat. Turn your meat as little as possible and abstain from forking. No, that's not a sexual term like spooning. Don't poke your steaks like a $10 hooker or they will lose their natural juices. After a set amount of time on one side, you will want to flip your steaks with the tongs. Cook for approximately the same amount of time as the first side and you should be good to go.

Step 5: Time it to perfection. Rare steaks should be cooked for approximately 5 minutes on each side, medium steaks for around 7 minutes on each side, and well-done steaks for approximately 10 minutes on each side. The times could be longer or shorter based on the thickness of your steak, so cooking times may vary.

Step 6: Poke your meat. You will want to pay attention to the internal temperature of the steaks to ensure that they are fully cooked. Using a meat thermometer, stick it in the thickest part of your steaks. The temperatures should be as follows: A medium rare steak should have an internal temperature of approximately 135 degrees Fahrenheit, a medium steak should be approximately 140 degrees Fahrenheit, and a well-done steak should be approximately 150 degrees Fahrenheit.

Step 7: Let em' sit then serve. Once they are cooked, let your steaks take a breather for a few minutes. This should keep its juices from running all over your cutting board as you go to serve your masterpiece.

Steak on a gas grill:

Step 1: Let your steak relax. Take your steak out of the fridge and let it sit for a while to come up to room temperature.

Step 2: Prepare to grill. Open the barbecue hood, turn your gas grill on high, ignite the burners, and start to prep your steak. You may want to brush the sides with olive oil and throw on any seasonings of your choice.

Step 3: Slap the steak on the grill. Throw the steak on the grill and cook each side for the same amount of time. Once complete, it should be a nicely cooked piece of meat.

Step 4: Pay attention to the time. Flip your steak and continue to grill it to your liking. Rare steaks should be cooked for approximately 5 minutes per side, medium steaks for around 7 minutes per side, and well-done steaks for approximately 10 minutes per side. The times could be longer or shorter based on the thickness of your steak, so cooking times may vary.

Step 5: Watch the internal temperature. Stick a meat thermometer in the thickest part of the steak to ensure that it is cooked all the way through. A medium rare steak should have an internal temperature of approximately 135 degrees Fahrenheit, a medium steak should be approximately 140 degrees Fahrenheit, and a well-done steak should be approximately 150 degrees Fahrenheit.

6

HOME IMPROVEMENT ADVICE

I. How to Change a Smoke Detector

Smoke detectors are a must have in every home. If one happens to crap out on you, you should hopefully be able to put on your big boy panties and change it yourself after reading this section.

Step 1: Grab a replacement. You will need to have a brand new smoke detector on hand (or a few if you are replacing all of them in your home) as well as a screwdriver.

Step 2: Don't get electrocuted. Shut off the power to the section of the home you will be fussing with. You will be playing with wires later on.

Step 3: Dismantle the old smoke detector. Remove the old smoke detector by turning it counter clockwise. You will notice that there is wiring running from the smoke detector to your ceiling (image on next page). Disconnect these wires. You will then have just the base plate connected to the ceiling. Remove the plate using a screwdriver.

Step 4: Remove your nut. Once the base plate is removed, the wires of the previous smoke detector will still be connected to the wiring in the ceiling via a wire connector, otherwise known as a wire nut. Simply unscrew the wire nuts to remove the old wiring. It is imperative that you turned off the power to avoid getting electrocuted to death.

Step 5: Match the wires. Check your new smoke detector for new wiring. Match the wires of the same color and connect them with a wire connector. Wires should connect as follows: Black to black and white to white. There will be a third wire present (most likely green in color) in both the ceiling and on the new smoke detector. Connect these wires together.

Step 6: Mount the new smoke detector. Once the wires are connected, mount the base plate that came with your new smoke detector. After the base plate has been attached, connect the wiring to your smoke detector and mount it by turning it clockwise onto the base. This step is illustrated at the top of the next page.

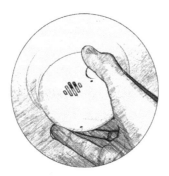

Step 7: Make sure it works. Turn the power back on and test your new smoke detector by holding down the test button. The detectors in your house should sound. This will indicate that you aren't as useless as your parents thought. Oh, and that you also installed your smoke detector successfully.

II. How to Change a Smoke Detector Battery

Do you ever hear a relentless chirping in your home and wonder what the hell it is? It is you failing to responsibly change the batteries to one, if not all, of your smoke detectors. If you don't feel like burning alive in your home without warning, feel free to peruse the steps below on how to change a smoke detector battery.

Step 1: Get a battery that lasts. Do some research and find out what type of battery your smoke detector requires. I personally haven't seen one that requires something other than a 9 volt but then again, I haven't seen two men butt fucking and that exists. Also, be sure to buy a quality 9 volt battery that will last more than a month. No one wants to hear the incessant chirping of a smoke detector because their batteries are too cheap.

Step 2: Locate the battery compartment. It should be on either the back or side of the smoke detector and accessible via a latch. If you feel nervous about playing with hard-wired electronic devices, feel free to shut off your power for this one although it is hardly necessary.

Step 3: Reveal the battery. Open the compartment to expose the old battery.

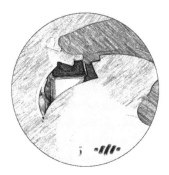

Step 4: Remove the old battery. Take the old battery out and use those grubby little sausage fingers to insert the new battery in its place (image on next page).

Step 5: Make sure it works. Close the compartment and hold the test button down until you hear chirping. If you do not hear chirping, either you're deaf or the battery was installed incorrectly.

III. How to Clean Out Your Rain Gutters

Cleaning out your rain gutters is a simple task that every young adult and homeowner should be capable of performing. You only need a few tools to accomplish the job and it can save you a wad of cash simply by putting in an hour or so of effort.

Step 1: Gather your equipment. While you're going to need a bucket, ladder, gloves, and a hand-held tool such as a trowel, you may also want to wear a tattered long sleeve shirt and some raggedy pants.

Step 2: Place your ladder. Depending on the kind of ladder you are using, position your ladder against or next to the gutters on your roof. If you happen to own an extension ladder, you may want to use a standoff stabilizer to refrain from damaging your gutters.

Step 3: Proceed to remove vast amounts of gunk. Using the trowel or tool of your choice, simply begin to remove the vast array of shit that has piled up in your gutters over time. To avoid moving the gunk from your gutters to your driveway, use the bucket as a receptacle during the process.

Step 4: Flush the system. The final step requires flushing out the remaining gunk using a hose. Be sure to flush all of your gutters as well as the downspouts with water to clear any leftover debris.

IV. How to Paint a Room

Odds are if you purchase a home you will want to spruce things up a bit by painting a few rooms. While hiring a professional can make the job easy and less time-consuming, it also costs a pretty penny. Instead, I advise you try your hand at painting on your own. Below you will find how to prep and paint a room like a sub-standard professional with Parkinson's. Keep in mind that there are a plethora of ways to go about painting a room. If you happen to like a different method, have at it.

Step 1: Preparation. Cover your floor with a drop cloth or old, cum-stained bed sheets to prevent getting paint all over your carpet. Remove the faceplates from your outlets and switches. If necessary, remove or cover any ceiling fans that may get in the way during the painting process as well. Last but not least, clean the areas that you will be painting. This consists of wiping the walls down with a damp rag and ensuring that all areas are clear of dust or debris that may diminish the quality of the paint job.

Step 2: Prime if needed. While primer isn't always necessary, it is useful if you happen to be making a drastic change in color. It may also be useful if you're painting drywall, repaired sections of a wall, or looking to create a glossy finish.

Step 3: Purchase the necessary materials to begin painting. You will most likely need the following: Paint, an array of paint brushes, a paint roller, a paint tray, and painter's tape. If you want to go the extra cautious route, grab yourself a mask, gloves, and goggles while you're at it.

Step 4: Protect your shit from splash damage. Put painter's tape on anything and everything that you want to protect from paint. Typically this will include window edges, ceiling edges, base molding, switches, outlets, and door hardware.

Step 5: Ventilate and start edging. Once you are prepared to paint, pop open the paint can(s), stir the paint with a wooden paint stick, and get to work. Open plenty of windows as well to allow the room to dry while avoiding the inhalation of paint fumes in the midst of your project. Start on the walls by painting the edges. This part will require a brush instead of a roller. You will want to dip approximately 1/3 of the brush into the paint. When painting, be sure to hold the brush like you're writing with a pencil. Stroke the brush gently along the edges while attempting to get as little paint on the trim as possible. If you're looking to paint the trim the same color, then forget it. Repeat the process until the entirety of the room has been completed.

Step 6: Prep your roller. Pour some paint into your tray. Grab your roller, dip it in the tray, and cover the entire roller head. Don't douse the roller in paint as it will make your carpet look like a murder scene. Simply give it a light coat of paint that will go smooth on the wall.

Step 7: Tackle the walls. Without getting paint on the ceiling, use the paint-covered roller to perform a "w" or zigzag pattern along the wall. When you become light on paint, simply give the roller another dip. You don't want to squeeze every last drop out of the roller while painting as this will cause you to actually soak up wet paint that has already been applied to the wall. You don't want to have to give the room more coats than needed when all is said and done, so be generous with the paint to begin with.

Step 8: Roll out some final touches. Once the entirety of the walls have been painted, use the roller and a brush to make any final touch-ups. Let it dry and you're good to go.

V. How to Plunge a Toilet

Remember your shit that was so large you had to show your friends to relish in the glory? Well, that asshole-splitting turd clogged your pipes and it is your responsibility to fix it. Luckily, you won't have to wallow in your own excrement for too long if you follow the three simple steps outlined below.

Step 1: Prepare for war. Grab a plunger and some gloves because you are about to have the battle of a lifetime. Keep in mind that a heavy-duty plunger with a flap that folds out from the cup will be more effective than its more simple, solely cup-shaped brethren.

Step 2: Submerge the plunger. Place the head of the plunger in the toilet to let it fill with water and not air. Once completed, use the plunger head to create a tight seal with the toilet bowl.

Step 3: Plunge like your life depends on it. Once the seal has been created, slowly push the plunger down and pull it right back up. This motion should begin to loosen any poo or toilet paper currently clogged in the pipe. If unsuccessful, continue to repeat the motion until the toilet becomes unclogged.

VI. How to Reset a GFCI Outlet

There are times where you may find yourself wondering, "why the fuck isn't this outlet working?" GFCI stands for ground fault circuit interrupter. They stop the flow of electricity to a certain outlet when an imbalance occurs. They can often be found in bathrooms, kitchens, laundry rooms, or garages. Restoring the flow of electricity to a GFCI outlet is simple and it sure as hell doesn't require an electrician to fix it. Outlined below are simple steps to remedy your problem so you can go back to charging your dildos and shaving those 80's porno pubes.

Step 1: Locate the affected GFCI outlet. It should have both a "test" and "reset" button on the face of the plate. If the GFCI needs to be reset, you will notice that the "reset" button is protruding from the outlet.

Step 2: Unplug your electronics. Turn off or unplug all appliances that are connected to the outlet as you do not want to harm them during the reset.

Step 3: Push it real good. Push in the "reset" button. Yes, it's that simple. For you visual learners, an image has been provided at the top of the next page for your convenience.

Step 4: Check the outlet. Plug in or turn on your appliances to check for a flow of electricity. They should work once more. If not, the problem may lie with your home's circuit breaker. For more information regarding circuit breakers, see the next section of this chapter.

VII. How to Reset a Circuit Breaker

Chances are at some point you will experience a tripped circuit in your home. Much of the time, people call handymen to fix this simple problem. Sadly, it probably takes them longer to process your bill than to reset the circuit. Below you will find the simple steps to resetting a tripped circuit if you ever find yourself without power to a certain section of your home.

Step 1: Assess the situation. If you lost power in part of your home, check to make sure the issue isn't with a GFCI (ground fault circuit interrupter) outlet. These outlets simply need you to press a "reset" button to get them to kick in. As stated in the previous section, they can be found on certain outlets near water, which usually include your kitchen, bathroom, laundry room, or garage.

Step 2: Check your box. If the GFCI isn't your problem, it's time to check your service box. This electrical service panel is usually located in the garage, on the side of the home, or in the basement if you happen to have one.

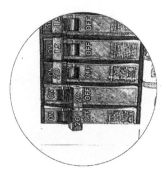

Step 3: Flip that switch. Open the service box and locate the tripped breaker. You will notice that the affected breaker is in an "off" position. In order to reset it, you need to ensure that it is *fully* turned to the off position. Once that has been completed, flip it completely on and power should be restored. If you need a visual, be sure to check out the image at the top of the next page.

Step 4: Repeat if necessary. If the power doesn't seem to come back on, attempt to turn the switch all the way off and back on once more. Your problem should be resolved.

VIII. How to Turn Off the Power to Your Home

This section is similar to the section entitled, "How to Reset a Circuit Breaker" in that they both require access to the electrical service panel in your home. This function is useful when performing certain repairs on electrical appliances in your home. It essentially requires the flip of a switch as described in the steps below:

Step 1: Locate your panel box. The electrical service panel is usually located in the garage, on the side of the house, or in the basement depending on the build of your home.

Step 2: Open the box to expose the breakers. You will notice that there are two types of breakers: a main breaker that controls electrical flow to the *entire* home and branch circuit breakers that control electrical flow to *parts* of the home.

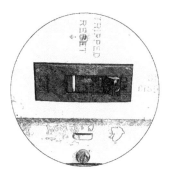

Step 3: Shut the power off. To shut off the power to your entire home, simply flip the main breaker to the "off" position. Upon doing so, all electrical flow to your home will cease. You should be free to work on any electrical devices or wiring as needed. To see this step in action, simply look to the top of the next page.

Step 4: Turn it back on. To restore your home's power, simply flip the main switch back into the "on" position. You should be good to go.

IX. How to Turn Off a Toilet's Water Flow

Your massive dookie just clogged the toilet and a delicious mixture of feces and H_2O is about to flow onto the floor. Luckily for you, a relative bought you this book on how to get learned good. Follow the simple steps below to shut off the water to your toilet.

Step 1: Find your water flow valve. Look in the back of your toilet and locate the pipe that leads from the toilet to the wall.

Step 2: Fondle your knob. The pipe should contain a valve. Grab the knob gently and move on to step three.

Step 3: Rotate the valve. Softly turn the valve clockwise until the flow of water ceases or until you feel as though the valve is shut (image on next page). Don't man-handle it as too much force may create a crack in the pipe.

Step 4: Restore the flow. To restore the flow of water to your toilet, simply turn the valve counterclockwise to its original state.

X. How to Turn Off the Water to Your Home

So you went to shut off the water to your toilet and cranked the valve so hard it snapped, causing water to leak all throughout your home. You need not worry. For emergencies such as this one, the step-by-step guide below explains how to shut off the water to your home.

Step 1: Locate your home's water shutoff valve. Traditionally it is located near a water heater, in the garage, or around the front of the home. When you locate a pipe that jets out of the ground and leads into your home, you've found it.

Step 2: Turn that bitch off. Once you have located the valve, turn it clockwise with either your hand or a wrench to shut it off. This should stop the flow of water to your home.

Step 3: Let it flow once more. To restore water flow, simply turn the valve counterclockwise and you should have flowing water in your home once more.

XI. How to Turn Off the Gas to Your Home

Your gas line snapped and now you have a leak on your hands. Instead of huffing gas like it's a fresh batch of glue, you can grow the fuck up and turn off the gas to your home using the steps below. However, before we get there, I have a few words of warning. Do not shut off the gas to your home unless you smell gas, hear gas escaping, see a broken gas line, or suspect a gas leak. Once the gas is shut off at the meter, do not try to turn it back on yourself. If the gas service shutoff valve is closed, your gas company or another qualified professional should perform a safety inspection before the gas service is restored and any appliance pilots are lit.

Step 1: Locate the shutoff valve and gas meter. The gas meter as well as the gas service shutoff valve are usually located on the side of your house, typically near the electrical meter. For all you apartment dwellers, the gas meter may be located in a cabinet enclosure built into the building. In these cases, the gas service shutoff valve can be located outside on a section of gas service pipe next to the building, or near the gas meter.

For you people that have crappy jobs and can't afford a house, there may be multiple meters serving gas to various units within a building. If that's the case, there will be individual gas service shutoff valves for each unit near each of the gas meters. You should also see a master valve for the entire building. Don't fuck with it. Instead, if you live apartment 69, find the gas meter with 69 written on it. If you have issues, your property manager or landlord might be able to help you locate your unit's valve.

Step 2: Shut off the gas. Using a twelve to fifteen inch adjustable pipe or crescent-type wrench, give the valve a quarter turn. The valve is closed when the part you put the wrench on, called a tang (not to be mistaken for poontang), is perpendicular to the gas pipe.

XII. How to Turn Off the Gas to Your Appliances

Inside your home you will find a variety of appliances that run on gas, such as water heaters, stoves, ovens, fireplaces, clothes dryers, and heating systems. If one decides to break on you like a cheap ass toy from China, you may need to shut the gas off before your home becomes the Hindenburg. Now, instead of listing the various ways to shut off the gas for multiple manufacturers and their respective appliances, I have provided a simple two step overview:

Step 1: Locate the shut off valve on the appliance. Most gas appliances have a gas shutoff valve located on the gas pipe leading to the appliance itself.

Step 2: Turn the valve in order to shut off the flow of gas. In most cases, a quarter turn will do. Once completed, the valve should be perpendicular to the gas line.

In most cases you will need to shut off the gas to an appliance if it is in need of repair or a replacement. If a shutoff valve is not present on some appliances in your home, getting them installed may be a good idea. Other than that, try not to blow your ass up while making any necessary repairs in your home.

XIII. How to Fix a Stuck Stove Igniter

911 Dispatcher: "Hello 911, state your emergency."

Dumb Shit to 911 Dispatcher: "The igniter on my gas stove keeps clicking no matter where I put the knob. I think my house is going to explode!"

911 Dispatcher to Dumb Shit: "Do you smell gas?"

Dumb Shit to 911 Dispatcher: "Yeah, my roommate just shit his pants because he is so scared."

911 Dispatcher to Dumb Shit: "Have you tried unplugging the stove?"

Dumb Shit to 911 Dispatcher: "Unplug... it's a gas stove."

911 dispatcher to Dumb Shit: "Okay, then what the fuck do you want me to do about it?"

Dumb Shit to 911 Dispatcher: "Send the fire department. They fix everything."

Don't be like the imbecile above. I know it's hard to imagine, but a gas stove igniter works the same way as a gas barbecue igniter: with a power source. While a barbecue igniter gets its electricity from a battery, a gas stove igniter gets its power from the electricity in your home. Just because you have a gas or LP/LPG (liquefied petroleum gas) stove doesn't mean that the stove works solely on gas or a flux capacitor. Before you were swimming in your dad's balls, gas stoves had utilized a pilot light that continually burned. That flame would then light the burner when the burner was turned on. Due to lack of energy efficiency, the pilot light was replaced by a spark igniter that is powered by electricity.

The igniter works the same way as a spark plug in a car. Essentially, a current in the igniter jumps across a gap from the igniter to the base of the burner, thus igniting the gas and subsequently, the burner itself.

Step 1: Shut it down. If your gas igniter is stuck, simply unplug the stove. After doing so, the clicking should cease immediately. Now, realize that you will not be able to melt your plastic army men on the burner until the igniter is fixed.

Step 2: Hire a professional. You will now either need to replace, clean, or fix the igniter. My advice? Call a repairman. If the fire department arrives at your location because you thought the house was going to explode, they're going to unplug your stove, tell you to call a repairman, and talk shit about you while they drive back to the station to prepare for a real emergency.

7

MISCELLANEOUS ADVICE

I. How to Address an Envelope

If you address an envelope wrong, odds are the intended recipient is never going to get that card or letter. To spare you from looking like an idiot, the essentials for addressing an envelope can be found in the simple steps below.

Step 1: The recipient's address. Write down the recipient's address in the center of the envelope on the front side. The first line should include the name of the person to whom the envelope is for. The second line should include the street address. Finally, the third line should include the city, state, and zip code.

Step 2: Your address. Write your return address in the top left-hand corner on the front side of the envelope. In the event that your envelope cannot be sent to the recipient, the postal service can send the letter back to you. Write your name, address, city, state, and zip code in the same manner as the recipient's address.

Step 3: Add a postage stamp. Purchase a postage stamp and place it in the top right-hand corner on the front side of the envelope. The postal service you choose to utilize isn't a fucking charity. If you forget the postage stamp, you're basically shit out of luck because like all things, the postal service costs money and that stamp is your envelope's ticket to where it needs to go.

Step 4: Send it out. Stick your envelope in an outgoing mailbox and it will be on its way.

II. How to Become More Organized

This section may seem a little vague and that's because it is. Anyone can become more organized if they utilize certain tools or learn to prioritize in a manner that works for them. You're probably thinking, "what the fuck does this guy know about organization?" During college I was taking up to 24 units a semester while captaining my collegiate soccer team. Mobile applications, note cards, and lists made a world of difference for me. It's about finding what works and implementing these things into your daily routine.

Tip 1: Create lists. Make one for the day so you have a better idea of what needs to be accomplished. Not only will you not forget to complete certain tasks, but it will also help you to prioritize. If jerkin' your gerkin' comes before homework or meetings, you may have a slight issue. Personally, I like to create a list for my day as well as my week, that way if I happen to complete my tasks listed for today, I can start chipping away at tomorrow. I also like to write my lists in order of importance. For example, a group project would come before chores and staring at tits on the internet.

Tip 2: Make technology your bitch. Utilize applications on your computer or cell phone. I recommend using both a sticky note app and an electronic calendar. The calendar is useful because it alerts you on when certain tasks are due or need to be accomplished. Not only that, but you can see what is coming weeks down the road. As far as the sticky note app is concerned, I place it on the home screen and use it as a to-do list. Because it is on the home screen, I see what still needs to be done for the day whenever I open up my mobile device or laptop.

Tip 3: Utilize the internet. If you work in groups, use free online software applications to complete your work. Fuck meeting in person. Not everyone has the same schedule and you always have that douche bag in the group that "will be there soon" but ends up never showing. With online file sharing applications, you can literally edit a paper or spreadsheet with other people at the same time while in different parts of the world. Use technology to your advantage.

Tip 4: Reflect on your daily routine. Step back and analyze how your time is spent. If porn, binge watching TV shows, and eating take up a majority of your day, you might have both diabetes and prioritization issues. Cut some of that shit out and use the extra time to knock out more tasks, hit the gym for an hour, or do something of value.

III. How to Set the Table

You're wanting to put on a formal dinner for a party or a significant other, but you have no clue where the plates, glasses, or utensils should go. That is quite alright, as the steps below walk you through setting up a table fit for impressing the in-laws.

Step 1: Gather your dinnerware. You will need the following: Salad forks, dinner forks, knives, butter knives, spoons, napkins, soup bowls, dinner plates, bread and butter plates, saucers, coffee cups, and wine glasses. If you take a look at the images on the following pages, you will find that it's easier than it sounds.

Step 2: Soup bowls and plates. Place the soup bowl on top of the dinner plate and set it directly in front of where your guests will be seated.

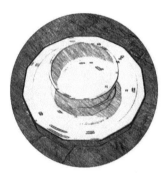

Step 3: Forks. Place the salad fork and dinner fork on the far left side of the dinner plate with the salad fork on the left-hand side.

Step 4: Spoons and knives. Place the knife and spoon on the right-hand side of the dinner plate with the spoon on the far right-hand side.

Step 5: Bread plates. Place the bread and butter plate directly above the forks. Lay the butter knife across the top of the plate.

Step 6: Coffee cups and saucers. Place the coffee cup on top of the saucer and directly above the spoon and knife.

Step 7: Wine glasses. Place the wine glass or glasses to the left of the coffee cup.

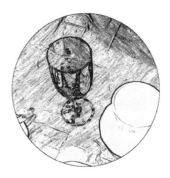

Step 8: Napkins. If there is soup being served, place a neatly folded napkin in-between the soup bowl and dinner plate mentioned in step 2. If there is no soup being served, place the napkin on top of the dinner plate.

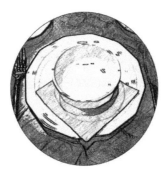

Your table is now ready to go. Sit back, relax, and eat like a king.

IV. How to Tip Properly

This section is short and sweet because it has only two points to cover. Find out why a dollar tip makes people look like skanks and if you're a waiter, why you shouldn't give shitty service.

Tip at least 15% of your total bill. If you were smart and used a coupon, tip on what the cost of your meal would have been without the coupon included. There is some reasoning behind this statement. In some regions, restaurants can pay their waiters and waitresses less than minimum wage due to the fact that they receive tips on their shifts. Without tips, there is a good chance they are surviving on poverty-level wages. If you received adequate service, please compensate the waiter or waitress for their efforts.

With that being said, it is unprofessional for waiters and waitresses to give poor service while at the same time expecting a substantial tip. The notion that tips are expected is absolutely absurd. Poor service does not constitute additional payment on my behalf simply because tips are expected in the United States. If you want to fuck me by neglecting my table, then I am going to fuck you on my receipt. So please, if you happen to be a waiter or waitress, serve your customers the way you would want to be served.

V. How to Be Polite

I would simply put, "don't be a dick," but that would be too vague. Simply be polite to those you do and do not know. Look at it this way, you never know what someone's situation is, so take the extra few seconds to not be an asshole and make both of your days a little better. Below you will find some tips on how to be a decent human being for once.

Tip 1: Hold the door. Hold the door open for strangers. It takes a couple seconds out of your day, and you avoid slamming the door in an old lady's face.

Tip 2: Open the car door for your woman. This one is for the men: Open the car door for your girlfriend or significant other. Are you going to suck your own dick? No, so among other things, it's the least you can do for your mate.

Tip 3: Say please and thank you. One thing I absolutely can't stand is when people refuse to say these simple words. It takes a second of your time and if you refuse to do so, you are modeling impolite behaviors for those around you.

Tip 4: Be tolerant of others. No one chooses to be a certain way. Gay men don't wake up one day saying, "you know what, today is the day that I am going to gargle cocks and take it in the ass." Genetic predispositions are everywhere in society. Do not judge people for who they are because 99% of the time, it does not affect you in any way, shape, or form.

Tip 5: If someone helps you out, return the favor. Let's say you need help moving or fixing up your home. Instead of kicking your friends out as soon as the job is done, splurge on some pizza and beer as a way to say thank you. The same thing goes when someone lets you borrow their vehicle. Fill up the tank before you return it. Otherwise, you may find yourself riding the city bus next time you need a ride.

Tip 6: Don't smoke in enclosed spaces. First off, carcinogens are being expelled into a confined area. Secondly, those cancer-causing carcinogens are now being inhaled by women, children, and others. Lastly, nearly everyone in the vicinity will end up smelling like shit for the remainder of the day.

Tip 7: Pay back borrowed monies. I am a stickler when it comes to money. If you borrow money from a relative or friend, fucking pay them back within the week. Don't play the whole, "but I gave you a ride last week" bullshit or anything of the sort. You borrowed money. You owe them money. Plain and simple.

Tip 8: Use headphones in public. If you feel the need to have a conversation or play a video on your mobile device while in public, do so while wearing headphones. Using your speaker phone in public is obnoxious.

The suggestions for how to be polite could become a book in and of itself. Don't talk when someone else is talking, chew with your mouth closed, speak in an appropriate tone for your audience, pay attention to speakers when they have the floor, turn off your phone when someone is giving a presentation, and don't be a snobby prick to employees because chances are, they hate their job. All in all, the moral of this section is that we should all try to be decent human beings. We don't see eye to eye on all matters, but that doesn't mean we can't be cordial and respect one another's opinions and differences. We are all living on the same planet, breathing the same, shitty air and eating food produced on the same farms. It's about time we start realizing that our actions impact the globe, not just ourselves.

AWW SHIT...

It looks like you've finished Grow the F*ck Up! If you loved what this book had to offer, please take the time to leave a 5-STAR review on Amazon, B&N, or any other site that you may have purchased it from!

Don't think it was 5-stars? Before you leave a review, reach out to me personally at thejohnkyle@gmail.com. If there happened to be something you didn't enjoy or maybe there is a how-to that you think is missing from the book, I would love to hear about it. I not only enjoy hearing from my readers, but I would also like to address any issues you may have with Grow the F*ck Up. So yes, that's my real email address and yes, I will respond to your messages even if you just want to tell me to go fuck myself.

ABOUT THE AUTHOR

John Kyle is a Master of Business Administration from the California State University educational system. Shortly after college, John realized that many young adults were incapable of performing the most basic of tasks in everyday life. Wanting to put a satirical spin on learning tasks and life lessons that were never taught in school, John decided to create Grow the F*ck Up. You can find more of his work by following John Kyle and Grow the F*ck Up on a variety of social media platforms.